MAYER SMITH

The Curse We Share

Contents

One

A Chance Encounter

Ava felt the rain before she heard it, a slow, steady rhythm tapping against the pavement. The city had become a blur, as if the world around her was painted in shades of gray and faded gold. She stood beneath the overhang of a small bookstore, watching the droplets fall, collecting in tiny pools before being swept away by the rush of wind. It was one of those moments when time seemed to stretch, when everything felt suspended—just long enough to notice the way the air tasted, cool and sharp, like it had something to say.

Her fingers grazed the corner of the weathered leather-bound book in her hands, the musty scent of its pages filling her senses. But as her gaze drifted across the street, she saw him.

He was standing just across from her, close enough to be part of the mist yet far enough to remain a stranger. There was something about him, something that made Ava's heart skip a beat. Maybe it was the way he stood, still, as if he was waiting for something—or someone. Or maybe it was the way the rain never seemed to touch him, as if he existed in a bubble, untouched by the world's harshness.

Her fingers tightened around the book in her hands, the leather creaking beneath her grip. She wanted to look away, to ignore the strange pull she felt toward him, but her body refused to obey.

The stranger's eyes locked with hers, and for a moment, the rain faded entirely. The streetlights blurred into soft halos of light. His gaze was intense, dark like the night, but there was something familiar about it, as if she had seen him before—or worse, as if she was meant to.

Ava shook her head, her breath coming out in a short, sharp exhale. What was she thinking? It was just some random guy. Her pulse quickened despite herself, and she forced her feet to move, stepping back toward the warmth of the bookstore. But before she could turn, something caught her eye.

There, on her palm, was a mark. A symbol.

Ava's heart thudded in her chest as she stared at it, confused. Her hand felt strange—like it was no longer entirely hers. The symbol was small, a series of intricate, interwoven lines that seemed to shift in the dim light, growing darker, sharper, as if alive. She blinked, but it didn't disappear. It pulsed under her skin, faint but undeniable.

The world around her seemed to tilt, and for a moment, she thought she might fall. She gripped the book tighter, focusing on its reassuring weight. But before she could register what was happening, the stranger crossed the street, moving with unnerving grace, like he was part of the rain itself.

"Hey," his voice was low, rough around the edges, like it had been a long time since he'd spoken. "Are you alright?"

Ava opened her mouth to speak but found the words tangled in her throat. How could he have known? Her eyes darted down to her palm again, but the symbol was gone, leaving only the faintest trace of heat. She rubbed her hand on her jeans, trying to erase it, but it wouldn't fade.

"I'm fine," she said, her voice shaking. It felt like a lie, but it was all she could muster.

He studied her for a long moment, his gaze never wavering. His expression was unreadable, but there was something in the way he looked at her that made her feel like he could see right through her, like he knew things she didn't even understand about herself.

"You're not fine," he said, his tone soft but certain. He stepped closer, and Ava instinctively took a step back, the cold air brushing against her skin. "The curse has already marked you."

Ava's breath caught in her throat, and she felt her pulse race, her mind spinning with confusion and fear. The curse? What was he talking about? But before she could voice her questions, he tilted his head slightly, as if listening to something only he could hear.

"You're not safe here," he continued, his voice quiet but urgent. "You need to leave. Now."

His words, laced with a strange authority, sent a chill down her spine. Ava wanted to deny him, to argue that she was fine, that this was just some random encounter with a stranger. But deep down, a part of her knew that wasn't true. There was something undeniable about the way he spoke, as if he knew something she didn't, something important.

"I—what do you mean?" Her voice barely reached above a whisper. She wasn't sure if she was asking him or herself.

He seemed to hesitate for a moment, his brow furrowing slightly, before he glanced at her with an unreadable expression. "I shouldn't have come here," he muttered under his breath, then his eyes met hers again, this time with an intensity that made her stomach flip. "I didn't want you to know yet."

Ava took a shaky step backward. She had no idea what was happening, but the strange, magnetic pull she felt toward him had grown stronger. Her body responded to him in ways she couldn't explain—desire and fear mixing in equal measure, creating a cocktail of confusion she didn't know how to drink.

"Who are you?" she asked, the question finally slipping past her lips.

The stranger didn't answer immediately. Instead, his gaze shifted to her palm once more, and for a second, she could have sworn the mark reappeared, shimmering faintly beneath his eyes. But when he looked at her again, it was gone.

"I'm… someone you'll need to trust," he said after a long silence. "Even if you can't understand why."

Ava swallowed, the words hanging heavy in the air between them. She wanted to ask so many questions—about the symbol, about the curse, about the connection she felt to him—but a knot in her throat prevented her from speaking.

"I don't know what you're talking about," she said instead, her voice unsteady.

The man sighed, as if he'd expected this. "It's not safe here anymore," he repeated, his voice urgent, low. "You have no idea what you've uncovered."

The sound of thunder rumbled in the distance, but Ava barely registered it. All she could focus on was the man standing before her, the one who seemed to know things she couldn't understand. The one who was too familiar, too strange, to be a random encounter.

"Please," he added, almost pleading. "Just trust me. Get out of here before it's too late."

She opened her mouth to protest, to ask more questions, but the moment she did, she heard a faint rustling behind her. It was the unmistakable sound of footsteps—too many, too quick. Someone was coming, and they weren't alone.

Her heart skipped a beat as panic surged through her veins. Without thinking, she turned to run, but the man's hand shot out, grabbing her wrist with surprising strength.

"Go," he commanded, his voice sharper now, his grip tightening. "I'll hold them off."

Ava didn't know who they were, but she didn't wait to find out. She pulled her arm free from his grasp, her feet moving on instinct, pounding against the rain-soaked pavement, her breath ragged in her chest. The streets blurred around her as she fled, but in the back of her mind, she couldn't shake the feeling that this wasn't over—not by a long shot.

Two

The Bloodline

Ava barely slept that night. She tossed and turned in the unfamiliar silence of her apartment, the echoes of the stranger's words ringing through her mind. "The curse has already marked you." Those words held a weight that sat heavy in her chest, gnawing at her even as the night stretched on. She couldn't shake the image of the symbol—so clear, so present on her palm—before it disappeared as quickly as it had appeared. She had never seen it before. Never. And yet, she couldn't ignore the instinctual feeling that it belonged there.

When morning finally arrived, it was gray and overcast, as if the clouds themselves shared her unease. She stood at the window for a long time, watching the rain dribble down the glass. The city was waking up slowly, people scurrying beneath umbrellas and overcoats, moving like ants beneath a blanket of fog. It felt like the world had been muted, like she was the only one awake, caught in a storm of her own making.

Her fingers twitched, itching for the book she had been reading yesterday. The leather cover felt reassuring in her hands, but it wasn't enough to calm the gnawing feeling in her gut. She needed answers, and the only way to get them was to find out more about what she had experienced—and what the stranger, Liam, had said.

The soft knock on her door startled her. She froze for a moment, her heart lurching in her chest. Who would be here this early? She wasn't expecting anyone.

Her hand hovered over the door handle, a surge of cold fear prickling her skin. It wasn't just the knock—it was the sense that whoever was on the other side had been watching her, had been waiting. Slowly, cautiously, she cracked open the door.

It was Liam.

He stood in the doorway, soaked from the rain, his dark hair damp and clinging to his forehead. His eyes locked with hers immediately, intense and unreadable, as if he could see straight through her. The moment he looked at her, a shiver ran down her spine.

"You didn't listen," he said, his voice rough, like it hadn't been used in days.

Ava didn't move. She wasn't sure what to say, wasn't sure what to do with the rush of emotions that surged through her at the sight of him. She should have slammed the door in his face. She should have told him to leave. But something about him, something in the way he stood there, made her feel like she was trapped in a world she didn't understand.

"Why are you here?" she finally asked, her voice barely a whisper, though she knew she was safe. Or at least, she hoped she was.

Liam stepped inside without waiting for her invitation, his eyes scanning the room. He was taller than she'd remembered, his broad shoulders filling the doorway, and yet there was an ethereal quality to him, as if he didn't quite belong. Like he was made of something other than the ordinary.

"I've come to help," he said. "You're in danger."

Ava's breath caught in her throat. "Danger?" she repeated, though she knew exactly what he meant. The curse. The mark. Her bloodline.

Liam nodded, his expression darkening. "Yes. It's already begun."

Ava's mind raced, trying to put the pieces together. She didn't want to believe him, didn't want to believe that something as impossible as a curse was real, but the fear in his voice made her doubt her own skepticism.

"I don't understand," she said, the words tumbling out in a rush. "What does this curse have to do with me? What is it? Why me?"

Liam hesitated before answering, his eyes flicking to the side, as if weighing the cost of telling her the truth. Finally, he spoke, his voice low, a little more vulnerable than she had heard it before.

"It's tied to your bloodline. A curse that's been passed down for centuries, starting with your ancestors," he said, pausing to look at her with an intensity that made her heart race. "It's not just some myth or superstition. It's real. And it will kill you."

Ava recoiled slightly, feeling the words cut into her like a knife. She backed away from him, retreating into the dim light of her apartment, trying to process what he had just said. Her mind was a fog, a haze of disbelief, but deep down, something inside her wanted to believe him. The way he said it, with such raw certainty, stirred something in her—a memory, perhaps, a feeling that she couldn't quite grasp.

"No," she said, her voice sharp, but the quiver in it betrayed her. "This is crazy. You're—"

She stopped herself before finishing the sentence, because something about Liam felt too real, too grounded to dismiss. He was here, standing in her apartment, soaked from the rain, with a look in his eyes that told her he had seen the darkness that lay ahead.

"I'm not crazy, Ava," he said quietly, as if reading her thoughts. "I know this is hard to believe, but I've seen it before. The mark. The way it pulses. It's calling you. It's always been calling you."

Ava's fingers brushed her palm, as if to feel for the symbol again, but it wasn't there. It had vanished. Or had it?

"Why me?" she asked again, her voice breaking. "Why me?"

Liam stepped closer, his gaze softening for the first time since he had entered. He seemed to be battling something deep within, a storm she couldn't see but could feel.

"Because you're the one it's always been meant for," he said, his voice barely above a whisper. "The curse can only be broken by someone with your blood. It's why the symbol chose you."

Ava's pulse quickened, her mind spinning with this new revelation. "The symbol… it chose me?" The words felt foreign on her tongue, like something out of a dream, or perhaps a nightmare.

Liam's eyes darkened again, and he took another step closer, the air between them growing heavier with each passing moment. "The curse has been waiting for you, Ava. For your bloodline. And now that it's awakened, it won't stop until it gets what it wants."

Ava's breath caught in her throat as she watched him move toward her, her pulse racing, a mixture of fear and something else—something warmer—flooding her senses. She wanted to pull away, to tell him to leave, but she couldn't. Not now. Not when he was the only person who seemed to understand what was happening to her.

"I don't know what to do," she whispered, barely able to meet his gaze.

Liam reached out, his hand brushing hers. His touch was surprisingly warm, a contrast to the chill of the rain-soaked world outside. It sent a shock of awareness straight through her, making her heart race even faster. She was painfully aware of the way her breath hitched in her chest, the way the air between them seemed to hum with energy. But more than that, she was aware of the way her pulse quickened, of the pull between them that seemed almost magnetic.

"Don't worry," he said, his voice soft, reassuring despite the chaos surrounding them. "I'm here now. And I won't let it take you."

Ava wasn't sure what to believe anymore, but in that moment, as Liam's hand lingered near hers, she realized something. Whatever this curse was, whatever danger lay ahead, she wouldn't be facing it alone.

Three

Unraveling the Past

The library smelled of dust and old paper, the kind of scent that made Ava's skin crawl with the weight of time. She stood at the massive wooden door for a moment, her hand hovering over the polished brass handle, unsure if she was ready to walk inside. The building loomed before her like a sentient thing, ancient stone walls lined with shelves that seemed to stretch forever, a labyrinth of knowledge she had never before dared to enter.

She had no real reason to be here—no real idea of what she hoped to find—but she couldn't ignore the gnawing need in her gut. The truth was somewhere in these walls, hidden among the forgotten pages and half-whispered secrets. Ava wasn't sure if she was ready to confront whatever lay waiting for her, but something, or perhaps someone, was calling her to this place.

The heavy door creaked as she pushed it open, the sound echoing through the cavernous space. She stepped inside, her shoes clicking sharply against the cold, marble floor. The silence here was absolute, almost suffocating. A hushed stillness that pressed against her chest and settled in her bones. She took a deep breath, trying to calm the pounding of her heart, but the air felt thick, heavy with history.

Ava had no real plan, no specific books to search for. But her instinct told her this was where she needed to be. She wandered through the aisles, fingers brushing lightly over the spines of the books, feeling the ancient threads of knowledge beneath her fingertips. Each book seemed to hold a secret, a whisper of something lost to time, and Ava could almost hear the voices— faint, like ghosts, urging her to find what she was looking for.

It was only when she reached the back corner of the library that she stopped, her breath catching in her throat. There, in the farthest alcove, was an old, tarnished brass plaque affixed to the wall. The engraving was faded, almost impossible to read, but as she stepped closer, the words slowly became clear:

Bloodlines and Curses: The History of the Marked.

Ava's heart skipped a beat. She didn't know how she knew it, but she understood the significance of the words, the weight they carried. Her palm itched as though the symbol she had seen there was calling to her, reminding her that this was the key to everything.

The air seemed to shift as she pulled the heavy volume from the shelf. The leather cover was worn, the edges cracked with age, and as she opened it, the faint scent of ink and mildew wafted into her nostrils. She flipped through the pages, searching for something—anything—that would help her understand the curse, the bloodline, the symbol.

The book was filled with stories of the cursed, of families who had carried the mark through generations, each one suffering a fate far darker than the last. There were mentions of deaths, disappearances, betrayals—and always the mark, a symbol that seemed to appear out of nowhere, marking its victims as if it had chosen them.

As Ava read, her stomach churned with unease. The stories weren't just tales. They felt real. They felt personal.

One passage caught her eye. It was written in an almost illegible script, the ink smudged, as though the writer had been in a hurry. But the words burned through the page with an unsettling clarity:

The Curse of the Mark is bound by blood, by betrayal. Only one who carries it can break its chains. But to break the chains, one must face the darkness of their own bloodline.

Ava's hand trembled as she turned the page, but her breath caught when she saw the next line.

Beware, for the bloodline is never free. The Mark chooses, and the one it chooses will suffer the consequences.

She slammed the book shut, her pulse racing. She could hear the blood rushing in her ears, feel the heat creeping up her neck. This couldn't be real. This was too much. But the chilling sensation in her palm, the echo of the mark that had appeared there, told her otherwise.

A sudden sound broke the quiet. A footstep, light but unmistakable, echoed from the far end of the library. Ava froze. She wasn't alone.

She turned slowly, eyes darting to the entrance of the aisle. Her heart pounded in her chest, and she swore she could hear her own breath, too loud, too frantic. A figure emerged from the shadows, tall and quiet, his presence suffocating in its intensity.

Liam.

His dark eyes locked onto hers immediately, and Ava felt a jolt of recognition—a wave of something she couldn't quite define, like a collision of past and present, like she had always known he would find her here. But it wasn't just recognition. It was a deep, instinctual pull, a magnetic force that kept her rooted in place, her feet unwilling to move.

"Should've known you'd come here," Liam's voice was soft, but there was an edge to it, something dangerous that made the hairs on the back of her neck stand on end.

Ava tried to speak, but the words caught in her throat. What was he doing here? How had he found her?

"I don't understand," she whispered, her voice tight. "I thought you said I was in danger. Why are you here?"

Liam didn't answer right away. He stepped closer, his eyes scanning the room, as if making sure they were truly alone. Then he fixed his gaze back on her, his jaw tense, his expression unreadable.

"You shouldn't have come here," he said quietly, the words heavy with meaning. "This place… it's not safe."

Ava's pulse quickened, but her eyes narrowed in confusion. "What do you mean? This is just a library. How could it be dangerous?"

Liam's lips twisted into something that wasn't quite a smile, but something far darker. "Because the people who guard these secrets won't let you leave once you've uncovered them."

The words hung between them like a dark omen, and Ava's chest tightened with a mixture of fear and curiosity. "The curse… is that what they're guarding?"

He nodded, taking another step forward, closing the distance between them. There was an undeniable tension in the air, something that crackled with an intensity that made her skin prickle.

"I didn't want you to find out like this," Liam continued, his voice low, almost regretful. "I didn't want to drag you into it, but it's already too late. You've seen it. You've felt it. The mark is only the beginning."

Ava swallowed hard, the weight of his words settling over her like a thick fog. "I don't want any part of this," she said, though her voice faltered, betraying her uncertainty.

"I know," Liam said quietly, his eyes softening for the briefest moment, before the hardness returned. "But it's already part of you. And there's no going back now."

For a moment, neither of them spoke. The silence stretched between them like an invisible barrier, but the tension remained, heavy and suffocating. Ava wanted to move, wanted to break free from the hold he seemed to have on her, but she couldn't.

And then, as if drawn by some invisible force, Liam's hand reached out, brushing against hers. His touch was gentle but firm, sending a shock of warmth through her skin. She tried to pull away, but her body refused to listen.

"You don't have to face this alone," he whispered, his breath warm against her ear. "I'm here. I'll help you."

But Ava wasn't sure if she wanted his help. She wasn't sure if she could trust him. And yet, despite the voice in her head telling her to run, to leave, she felt herself drawn to him, as if the curse itself had already begun to tie them together.

Her breath caught in her throat. There was no escaping it now.

Four

Forbidden Ties

The sun hung low in the sky, casting a dim, golden light across the city as Ava made her way through the cobbled streets. The heavy fog from earlier had begun to lift, but the air still felt thick with something unspoken—something that lingered in the corners of her mind, something she couldn't quite grasp. She had barely slept the night before, and every time she closed her eyes, she saw the symbol, pulsing with an eerie light, glowing beneath her skin. It felt real, like it had been there for far longer than she had ever known, as if it had always been a part of her, waiting for the right moment to reveal itself.

Her hand trembled slightly as she adjusted the scarf around her neck, trying to distract herself from the strange pull that seemed to follow her wherever she went. It wasn't just the mark. It was everything. Liam. The way he had appeared in her life, the way he had so easily swept in, a stranger with too many answers, and yet, somehow, not enough.

She had no idea what to make of him—of them. Her thoughts were a tangle of confusion and desire, and each time he spoke, it was as though she was drawn further into a world she wasn't sure she belonged to. But the more she thought about it, the more she realized she had never truly belonged anywhere. Not before the mark. Not before him.

The door to the café jingled as she entered, the warm scent of freshly ground coffee and baked pastries filling the air. The low hum of conversation washed over her, but it barely registered in her mind. She was still lost in thought, her mind spiraling back to the cryptic warnings Liam had given her—the ones that had sent shivers down her spine. It's not safe. You can't trust anyone. His words had been urgent, but beneath the sharpness of his tone, there had been something else. Something more dangerous.

She shook her head, trying to clear the fog from her mind, but it didn't work. Liam's presence, his touch—those lingering moments of intimacy, those fleeting glances—they were enough to keep her from truly focusing on anything else. She ordered her coffee in a daze, not really hearing the barista's greeting, and moved to the far corner of the café, a small table by the window where she could watch the world pass by without being noticed.

But as she sat down, a familiar figure appeared in the doorway.

Liam.

He was drenched from the rain, the hem of his coat dark with water as he moved toward her, his gaze scanning the room as if he were searching for something—or someone. When his eyes met hers, the tension that had been building between them seemed to crackle in the air like electricity. Ava's breath caught in her chest, a rush of heat flooding her veins despite the cool air in the café.

"Mind if I join you?" Liam asked, his voice a mixture of reassurance and command.

Ava swallowed, her throat dry. She wanted to say no. She wanted to tell him to leave, to stop pulling her into this madness. But the words died on her lips as she nodded, unable to refuse him. He slid into the seat across from her, his presence too much—too commanding, too intense—and for a moment, neither of them spoke.

The silence stretched between them, thick with the weight of things left unsaid. Ava could feel the sharpness of his gaze, his eyes tracking her every movement, as though he could see past the walls she had built around herself. Her fingers curled around her coffee cup, the warmth of it offering little comfort as the chill from the rain seemed to seep into her bones.

"I didn't expect you to come," he said, finally breaking the silence. His voice was low, measured, but there was an edge to it now, as if something deeper was stirring beneath the surface.

Ava met his eyes, trying to steady herself. "I didn't expect you to follow me."

He smiled, but it was tight, strained. "I don't follow. I watch. It's safer that way."

The words hit her like a punch to the gut, and for the first time, she felt a shiver of fear crawl down her spine. Safer? What was he talking about? What was going on beneath the surface of this strange connection?

"I didn't ask for any of this," Ava said, her voice almost a whisper, barely audible over the soft murmur of the café. "I didn't ask for you. I didn't ask for any of it."

Liam's gaze softened, but there was something in his eyes— a flicker of something darker—that made Ava hesitate. She couldn't place it, but it made her heart race in a way that both terrified and excited her. "I know," he said quietly. "You didn't. But this… this is bigger than both of us. And you can't run from it."

She opened her mouth to argue, but the words faltered as a strange sense of inevitability settled over her. It was true. She couldn't escape it. No matter how hard she tried to fight it, the mark was already a part of her, and the mystery of her bloodline was starting to unravel in ways she couldn't control.

"Why me?" she asked, the question slipping out before she could stop herself. "Why did the mark choose me? What does it want?"

Liam's lips parted as if to respond, but then he hesitated. The silence that followed was heavy with the weight of secrets—things she wasn't ready to hear, things he wasn't sure he should tell her.

"It's not just the mark," he said, his voice low, almost too quiet. "It's the bloodline. Your family. They've been marked for generations, a curse that's been passed down from one to the next. There's a reason it chose you. Your blood is connected to something ancient, something dark."

Ava's pulse quickened, her heart pounding in her chest. She didn't want to believe him. She didn't want to think about the possibility that everything she knew about her life was a lie—that her bloodline was cursed, that she was bound to something out of her control. But the more Liam spoke, the more she couldn't deny the truth in his words.

Her fingers tightened around the edge of her coffee cup, the ceramic cool against her skin. "And what does that mean for me? What am I supposed to do with this… curse?"

Liam didn't answer right away. He reached across the table, his hand brushing lightly over hers. The touch sent a jolt of warmth through her, a spark that ignited something deep inside her—something she didn't fully understand. Her breath hitched in her chest, her body betraying her, but she couldn't pull away. Not yet.

"I don't have all the answers," he said, his voice rougher now. "But I know one thing. You're not alone in this. I'm here. And

I'm not going anywhere."

The intensity in his words made Ava's head spin. Her pulse hammered in her ears, and her body responded to him in ways that made her feel both alive and terrified. She wanted to fight him. She wanted to push him away, to scream that none of this made sense, but she couldn't. Not when his gaze held hers so firmly, not when everything in her screamed that he was the one person who could protect her from whatever was coming.

"You don't have to do this," Ava whispered, her voice barely audible, the words slipping past her lips before she could stop them. "You don't have to be here. You don't have to get involved in this."

Liam's face softened, but his eyes remained dark, intense. "I'm already involved, Ava. We both are. And there's no way out."

She stared at him, her mind racing with questions she didn't know how to ask, her heart caught in a web of desire, fear, and uncertainty. What was she supposed to do with this man? This stranger who knew her too well, who seemed to hold the answers to questions she hadn't even asked.

And yet, as the silence stretched between them, she realized something: she couldn't walk away from him. She didn't want to.

Five

Ghosts of the Past

The rain had returned, falling in sheets that seemed to blur the world beyond the windows, turning the city streets into a haze of shadows and light. Ava stood at the window of her apartment, her hands pressed against the cold glass, watching the water streak down like tears. The sound of the rain was a constant hum in the background, but her mind was elsewhere, far from the rhythm of the storm. It was still there—the mark. She could feel it under her skin, as if it had taken root and now pulsed with a life of its own. It was a constant, nagging reminder that her life had changed in ways she couldn't understand.

Ava turned away from the window, her heart pounding with the weight of everything that had happened since Liam had walked into her life. The stranger who had promised answers but only left her with more questions. Your bloodline is cursed, he had said. And somehow, she couldn't escape the feeling that this was just the beginning. She could still hear his voice in her head, that low, urgent tone, warning her that things were going to get much worse before they got better.

Her fingers brushed the back of her neck, where the skin still burned with the memory of his touch. She should have been afraid. She should have pushed him away when he had come so close, but she hadn't. Instead, something about him had felt so familiar, so unavoidable, that she had let him in. And now, here she was, standing in her apartment, staring out into the storm, knowing that whatever was coming, she couldn't hide from it.

Her phone buzzed, snapping her out of her thoughts. She glanced at the screen and saw Liam's name. Her pulse skipped a beat, and for a moment, she hesitated, unsure if she should answer. She had grown used to his presence, his quiet insistence on being a part of her life, but there was still a part of her that felt conflicted. Part of her wanted to shut him out, to retreat into the safety of her own world, but the other part—the part that was still so drawn to him—knew she couldn't. Not now.

She answered the call.

"Ava," his voice came through the speaker, low and steady, but there was something in it that made her stomach tighten. "I need you to come with me. There's something I need to show you."

Ava's heart skipped, a flicker of fear stirring inside her. "What is it? What's going on?"

"It's not safe," Liam replied. "Not here. Not anymore. You need to trust me. This is bigger than both of us."

She stared at the phone for a long moment, the weight of his words settling over her like a fog. Her mind screamed for her to refuse, to stay put, to ignore the pull he had over her. But she knew, deep down, that she had already crossed a point of no return. She wasn't sure what was happening, but she knew it had something to do with him. With the curse. And with the mark that burned like fire beneath her skin.

"Okay," she whispered, finally giving in. "I'll come."

The line went dead before she could say anything else, and Ava felt a strange sense of finality, as if she had just taken the first step into a world that would change everything she knew.

The car ride was silent, the only sound the faint hum of the engine as it cut through the rainy streets. Liam didn't speak, his hands gripping the wheel tightly, his eyes focused on the road ahead. Ava sat beside him, her hands clenched in her lap, her stomach a knot of anxiety. She couldn't shake the feeling that they were headed into something dangerous, something she wasn't prepared for.

The streets grew darker as they left the city behind, the buildings thinning out, replaced by a dense forest that seemed to swallow the road whole. The trees loomed on either side, their branches swaying in the wind, their shadows stretching long across the pavement. Ava's breath caught in her throat as the car turned onto a narrow, winding path that led deeper into the woods.

"Where are we going?" she asked, her voice quiet, her eyes scanning the darkened forest.

"A place I've been avoiding," Liam said, his tone distant, as if the answer didn't satisfy him any more than it did her. "But it's the only place that can tell you the truth."

Ava glanced over at him, her gaze lingering on his profile. His jaw was tight, his brow furrowed in concentration, and for a moment, she wondered just how much of this was planned. How much of this had he known all along?

The car slowed as they approached an old, dilapidated mansion that stood in the middle of the clearing. The house was massive, its once-grand architecture now crumbling and covered in ivy. The windows were dark, empty. There was a sense of abandonment, but there was something more to it—something that sent a chill racing down her spine.

"We're here," Liam said, his voice barely audible.

Ava opened her door, the damp air immediately hitting her skin as she stepped outside. The sound of the rain was muffled by the canopy of trees, but the air was thick with tension. She glanced at Liam, who was already walking toward the house, his footsteps steady, his figure disappearing into the shadows. Without thinking, Ava followed.

The front door creaked open as they approached, and the smell of must and decay hit her like a physical blow. The air inside was stale, heavy with dust, but there was something else—

something that made her skin crawl. The hairs on the back of her neck stood on end as she stepped over the threshold, her senses heightened, alert to every movement, every whisper of the wind.

"This place…" Ava murmured, her voice trembling. "What is this place?"

Liam didn't answer right away. He simply led her down a long, dark hallway, the walls lined with old portraits, their eyes seemingly following them as they moved. The floors creaked beneath their feet, the sound echoing through the empty space.

Finally, they reached a door at the end of the hallway, and Liam paused before pushing it open. The room beyond was dimly lit, filled with shadows, but as Ava stepped inside, her breath caught in her throat.

It was a study, but not like any study she had ever seen. The walls were lined with shelves filled with ancient books, their spines cracked and yellowed with age. There were dusty old maps spread across a large oak desk, their edges curling, and in the center of the room was a massive fireplace, the hearth cold and empty. But it was the book on the desk that drew her attention. The cover was dark, its surface etched with strange symbols that seemed to shimmer in the dim light.

Ava's heart pounded in her chest as she approached the desk, her fingers itching to touch the book, to open it and find the answers that had eluded her for so long. But before she could reach for it, Liam stepped forward, his hand resting lightly on her wrist, stopping her.

"Don't touch it," he said, his voice low, almost a warning. "That book is tied to the curse. It's part of your bloodline's past. Part of what's been hidden."

Ava turned to face him, her breath catching in her throat as she saw the look in his eyes—a mixture of fear and something darker. He was afraid. But of what?

"Why are you so afraid of it?" she asked, her voice barely a whisper.

Liam's eyes flashed with something unreadable, and for a moment, he said nothing. The silence stretched between them, thick and suffocating, until he finally spoke.

"Because it's not just a book, Ava," he said, his voice hardening. "It's a doorway. A doorway into the past. And if you open it, you might find things you're not ready to see."

Ava's pulse raced as she looked at the book again, her mind spinning with the weight of his words. She wanted to know the truth—she had to know—but she could feel the pull of danger, the warning in Liam's voice. The curse was real, and it was tied to her bloodline, but what would she uncover if she dared to open that door?

"I don't think you're ready to face it," Liam added, his voice quieter now, a note of regret in it. "But you will be. In time."

Ava turned away from the book, her chest tight with the weight of everything she had just learned. She didn't know if she was ready, but something deep inside her stirred, an undeniable force that pushed her forward. The curse was already a part of her, and there was no going back. Whatever the past held, she was going to have to face it.

And with Liam by her side, she would.

Six

Forbidden Ties

The rain had begun to thin into a steady drizzle as Ava stood in front of the massive wrought iron gates, her heart racing. They were no longer on the path back to the mansion where they had uncovered secrets that only left her with more questions. This time, they had driven deeper into the forest, the towering trees closing in around them like dark sentinels. The air was damp, the scent of moss and earth mixing with the sharp tang of pine.

Ava stood there, her fingers gripping the edge of her coat tighter as she looked at the towering gates in front of her. They were the last remnants of a place she knew existed, but never thought would actually be part of her life. The Larkin Estate.

"Are you sure about this?" she asked, her voice trembling despite her best efforts to sound confident.

Liam's gaze was steady as it met hers, his expression unreadable. The only sign of his internal struggle was the faint twitch in his jaw, the only crack in his calm facade. But she knew he was as uncertain as she was, perhaps even more so. There was a heaviness in the air tonight, a sense of something poised on the edge of breaking.

"You're the one who wanted answers," he said softly, the words laced with a quiet urgency that only she could hear.

"I didn't think it would lead me here," Ava replied, her voice more fragile than she intended.

He was already stepping forward, reaching for the rusted iron bars that separated them from the unknown. The gate creaked in protest as he pushed it open, the sound breaking the heavy silence that had hung over them since they'd arrived.

"You don't have to do this," Liam said, turning to face her. His gaze was softer now, more vulnerable, but his eyes still carried the same depth of intensity that made Ava feel as though he could see into the very core of her.

Ava hesitated, unsure of the right words. What was there left to say? The questions still gnawed at her mind, and she had no answers, only the overwhelming sensation that the only way out was through.

"I need to," she finally said, her voice quiet but resolute. "I need to know."

Liam nodded, his eyes flickering with something that might have been sadness, but it was gone too quickly for her to be certain. He stepped aside, motioning for her to follow, and despite the knot in her stomach, Ava moved. She didn't know why she felt this way—torn between the need to flee and the pull toward whatever dark force was drawing her in—but it didn't matter now. She was already too deep.

The path they walked down was narrow, flanked by overgrown ivy and tangled weeds that clawed at her ankles. The forest was suffocating in its closeness, the trees hanging overhead like a canopy, blocking out the last vestiges of daylight. It was hard to tell where the night began and where the shadows of the past lingered.

As they walked, Ava's thoughts were a whirlwind, swirling around the truth she had uncovered—the truth about her bloodline, the curse that clung to her as if it had always been a part of her, and the strange connection she shared with Liam. There was something more between them, something deeper than just shared secrets and dark histories, but it was tangled, clouded by the chaos of everything that had happened. Every time she tried to understand what they were, it only slipped further away from her grasp.

Suddenly, a low, guttural noise broke through her thoughts. Ava froze, her breath hitching in her throat. She turned to Liam, her eyes wide with fear, but he was already tense, his body stiff as he listened to the sound. The low growl came again, followed by the unmistakable rustle of movement.

Ava's heart hammered in her chest. "What is that?" she whispered.

Liam didn't answer immediately. His gaze flicked to the shadows ahead, his eyes narrowing in recognition. He seemed to be considering something for a moment, as if weighing a decision that carried heavy consequences.

"Stay close," Liam muttered, stepping forward with more urgency. "And keep quiet."

Ava's breath quickened as she followed him, her pulse thundering in her ears, but there was a cold dread creeping through her veins, seeping into her bones. She could hear the growling now, moving closer, a low, threatening sound that made the hairs on the back of her neck stand up.

Liam didn't slow his pace. He kept moving forward, his every step deliberate, like a predator sensing a threat just beyond the veil of sight. Ava's footsteps faltered, her heart racing faster as they approached a large stone structure, its towering silhouette emerging from the misty darkness ahead. The Larkin Estate.

The estate loomed before them, its façade looming like an old ghost, crumbling with age and neglect. The windows were dark, lifeless, but somehow, they seemed to watch them as they approached. There was a presence here, an energy that Ava could feel in the very air around her.

"Who—who lives here?" Ava asked, her voice trembling as she glanced over at Liam. She wanted to scream, wanted to run, but her feet wouldn't move.

"The Larkin family," Liam replied, his voice tight. "The curse you're tied to, it's tied to them. To their bloodline."

Ava's mind reeled. She wanted to ask more—how was she connected, what did that mean, why did she need to come here?—but the questions died on her lips as the growl grew louder, unmistakably close now. Something moved in the shadows ahead of them, a flash of dark fur.

"Liam…" Ava's voice broke, the words catching in her throat.

He grabbed her wrist, his grip firm, but his eyes—dark, urgent—met hers. "Trust me," he said, his voice soft but hard, full of an intensity she couldn't escape. "You have to trust me."

But trust him? With the growl growing louder and more menacing? With the truth about her bloodline—about the curse—that she was only starting to understand?

Before she could ask, the growl cut through the air again, closer this time. And then, in the span of a heartbeat, the creature lunged from the shadows—a monstrous wolf, its eyes glowing with an unnatural yellow light, its fangs bared in a snarl of hunger.

Ava screamed, pulling away, but Liam's hand was there, his grip unyielding as he yanked her closer to him, the space between them closing, their bodies pressed together. The wolf stopped just a few feet from them, its teeth glinting in the pale light of the moon. Its eyes were locked on her now, the air around them thick with a dark energy.

Liam stepped forward, his voice steady despite the danger. "You're not here for her," he said, his voice like steel. The wolf growled again, low and menacing, but it didn't move. Liam's eyes met Ava's, his gaze intense, desperate. "Ava, I need you to listen to me."

Ava couldn't think. Couldn't breathe. The creature before her was a nightmare, a primal force of nature, and it was staring her down, its eyes full of hunger and death. But even through the fear, she felt it—the connection between her and Liam, the bond that was pulling them closer.

"I'm here with you," Liam whispered, his lips brushing against her ear as he stepped forward again. His voice was soft, but there was a firm, unwavering certainty to it. "And we'll get through this. Together."

Ava nodded, her pulse racing. She had no idea what she was doing, no idea what had just happened, but she felt the warmth of Liam's presence, the strength of his grip, and the surety that, for the first time in a long while, she wasn't alone.

The creature took one more step back, its eyes still fixed on her, but it didn't approach again. Slowly, hesitantly, it turned and melted back into the shadows.

Ava exhaled in a breath she didn't know she had been holding, her legs trembling. But Liam's presence was like a shield, and she stayed close, leaning into him as he guided her into the mansion's dark depths.

The night was far from over, and neither of them knew what would happen next. But Ava knew one thing—there was no turning back now.

Seven

Shadows of Betrayal

Ava's breath came in ragged gasps, the chill of the night air biting at her exposed skin as she stumbled through the crumbling halls of the Larkin Estate. The echo of her footsteps seemed deafening in the silence, reverberating off the stone walls, but the oppressive stillness was only broken by the occasional creak of the house settling under the weight of the storm outside.

Her heart pounded, every instinct telling her to turn back, to run, but something—the pull of the curse, the feeling that everything in her bloodline had led her here—held her rooted to the spot. Her thoughts whirled, each moment with Liam becoming a twisting thread in a larger web of fear and desire. She wanted to pull away from him, from everything that was happening, but she couldn't. She wouldn't. Not when there was no way back, not when the danger was no longer just a possibility but a certainty.

Liam walked beside her, his presence at once a source of comfort and dread. His hand brushed against hers, just enough to send a shiver down her spine, though he made no attempt to hold her. He didn't need to. The connection between them was palpable, invisible but tangible, drawing them closer with each passing second.

"I told you it wouldn't be easy," Liam said, his voice low, steady despite the chaos swirling around them. His tone carried an edge, a quiet resignation that sent a chill down her back. Ava glanced at him, her pulse quickening at the intensity in his gaze. His eyes—always so dark, so filled with unspoken truths—seemed to cut straight through her.

"I never thought it would be easy," Ava whispered, her voice tinged with something she didn't fully understand. Fear. Curiosity. Something more. "But I didn't think it would feel like this."

Liam stopped abruptly, his eyes narrowing as he listened to something Ava couldn't hear. Her heart skipped a beat as the silence stretched between them, thick and suffocating. The storm outside raged against the windows, the wind howling through the broken panes, but there was something else—a distant sound, like footsteps. Footsteps that shouldn't have been there.

"Someone's coming," Liam muttered, his hand curling into a fist by his side. His jaw tightened, the muscles in his neck standing out in sharp relief.

Ava took a step closer to him, the adrenaline coursing through her veins. "Who? What's going on?"

His gaze flickered to the shadows, his expression unreadable. "We're not alone."

Before she could respond, the door at the end of the hallway creaked open, and a figure emerged from the darkness, moving with an almost unnatural grace. The figure was tall, cloaked in shadows, its features obscured by the dim light. But Ava could see the outline clearly enough. The air seemed to hum with an energy she couldn't explain.

The figure stepped forward, revealing itself in the soft flicker of candlelight. It was a woman, her face pale, almost ethereal in its beauty, but there was something unsettling about her presence. She was dressed in a dark, flowing gown that seemed to ripple around her like smoke, her eyes locking onto Ava with an intensity that made her blood run cold.

"So you've come," the woman said, her voice lilting, as though it were meant to be a song, but there was an underlying malice that made it sound like a threat.

Ava froze, a shiver running down her spine as the woman's gaze fixed on her. There was a sharp, unsettling familiarity about her, something Ava couldn't place but that felt like it had been haunting her for years.

Liam's hand shot out, grabbing Ava's wrist with surprising strength. His grip was tight, like a lifeline, pulling her back toward him. "No," he said, his voice laced with warning. "You're not supposed to be here."

The woman's lips curled into a smile, but it was cold, cruel. "I am the one who decides who belongs here, Liam," she said, her voice soft but edged with a razor-sharp finality. She stepped forward, her presence almost suffocating. The temperature in the room seemed to drop, the air turning frigid as if her very being sucked the warmth from the space.

"Who are you?" Ava found herself whispering, though she knew, deep down, that she didn't need to ask. She could feel it—the deep connection between this woman and the cursed history that now enveloped her.

The woman laughed, a sound like broken glass. "Ah, so you've figured it out already," she said, tilting her head slightly as she regarded Ava with a predatory gaze. "How convenient. You've come for the truth, haven't you?"

Liam stepped forward, his jaw tight, eyes burning with a mixture of anger and something darker. "Leave her out of this," he snarled, his voice low and dangerous.

But the woman simply smiled. "She's already involved, Liam. She always has been."

Ava felt a knot twist in her stomach. She had no idea who this woman was or how she knew Liam, but there was something deeply wrong about the situation. The woman's presence felt like a tightening noose, each word she spoke making the air grow heavier, more suffocating.

"What do you want with her?" Liam demanded, his voice trembling with barely-contained rage. "Why are you here?"

The woman's smile widened, but it wasn't one of kindness. It was the smile of someone who knew exactly what was coming. "She's my legacy," she said, each word dripping with venom. "Just as you are, Liam. We're all bound by the same blood, the same curse. You should have known she'd come for it. She's always been meant to take her place in this world."

Ava felt a chill crawl up her spine as the words sank in. Legacy. Blood. Curse.

Before she could react, the woman's eyes flickered to her palm, and Ava's breath caught in her throat as the mark she had tried so hard to ignore appeared once again, glowing faintly beneath her skin. It burned with a sharp intensity, sending a wave of heat through her body that made her gasp.

"No…" she whispered, backing away, trying to escape the overwhelming sensation. But it was too late. The mark pulsed again, stronger this time, as if it were alive—alive and demanding something from her.

"You're mine now," the woman said, her voice soft, coaxing. "You've always been mine, Ava. Your blood, your soul—they were always meant to be part of this."

Ava felt the room spin as the weight of the words sank in. She had been drawn into this—this twisted legacy—and now she was bound to it, whether she wanted to be or not.

Liam stepped forward, his face a mask of determination, and he pulled her closer to him, his body a shield between her and the woman. His grip was strong, his presence solid against the dark energy that seemed to bleed from the woman like poison.

"No," Liam said, his voice low and unyielding. "You're wrong. I won't let you have her. Not this time."

But the woman only laughed, the sound chilling, as she took another step forward. "You have no say in this anymore, Liam. None of us do."

Ava's heart was pounding in her chest as she clutched onto Liam, the mark on her palm still burning, still demanding. "Who are you?" she whispered, her voice hoarse, broken by fear. "What do you want from me?"

The woman's smile faded into something darker, something more calculating. "I want you to fulfill your destiny," she said, her voice almost sweet now. "I want you to take your rightful place. As the one who breaks the curse, or as the one who becomes part of it."

The words hung in the air like a curse in itself, thick and suffocating, and Ava could feel the weight of them pressing against her chest. She didn't know what her future held, but one thing was clear: whatever was happening, whatever twisted history this woman was part of, it was pulling her into a darkness she couldn't escape.

And with Liam standing beside her, she knew there was no going back.

Eight

The Test of Love

The wind had picked up again, howling through the trees outside, its eerie whistle threading through the cracks of the old mansion's stone walls. Ava stood by the grand fireplace, the flickering flames casting shadows that danced like specters across the room. Her hands, cold despite the warmth from the fire, were clasped tightly in front of her, her mind racing with every possible question she hadn't been able to ask. Her eyes drifted to Liam, who stood just a few feet away, his gaze focused on the hearth but his thoughts clearly elsewhere.

It had only been hours since the woman, the stranger who had claimed Ava was part of a legacy that stretched back centuries, had disappeared into the shadows of the mansion. The encounter had left Ava shaken to her core, her bloodline suddenly not just a mystery but a horror she could no longer ignore. And the mark… that symbol that burned on her skin, pulsing with a life of its own, a constant reminder that there was no turning back now.

But more than the curse, more than the revelation of the twisted bloodline that bound her, there was Liam. And every time she looked at him, something inside her pulled tighter. A mixture of fear, desire, and uncertainty, all entwined into one. She didn't know what to do with it.

"Ava," Liam's voice cut through her thoughts, soft but edged with urgency. She turned to him, her heart skipping at the way his eyes found hers immediately, as though he had been waiting for her to meet his gaze.

"Are you alright?" he asked, his voice low and filled with something unspoken.

She nodded, though the tremor in her hands betrayed her. "I'm fine," she replied, her voice barely above a whisper. But she wasn't fine. Not really. She couldn't remember the last time she'd felt truly fine—when had everything in her life stopped making sense?

Liam stepped closer, his presence suddenly filling the space between them, his figure casting a shadow that seemed to stretch endlessly against the walls. Ava's breath hitched as he reached out, his hand brushing against her arm, his touch light but electric. It was as if the contact sent a shockwave through her, her heart racing, her mind spiraling with a thousand thoughts.

"Liam…" she began, but the words tangled in her throat. She didn't know how to ask the questions, how to voice the fear that gnawed at her. She didn't know what she was supposed to feel anymore—for him, for herself, for this cursed path she was now walking.

He didn't speak at first, simply watching her, as though weighing his own emotions, his own fears. And then, almost imperceptibly, he stepped even closer. The air between them felt charged, as if every second spent not touching was a second wasted. She could feel his breath now, warm against her skin, and her pulse quickened with the awareness of how close they were.

"You're scared," Liam said finally, his voice softer now, a low murmur that seemed to pull at her heartstrings. "I can see it in your eyes, in the way you stand here, waiting for something you don't know how to face."

Ava swallowed, her throat dry. "I don't know what to do," she admitted, her voice cracking, the truth slipping out in a way she hadn't meant for it to. "I don't know what's happening to me."

Liam's gaze softened, his thumb gently brushing the back of her hand, and for a moment, everything else faded away. The storm outside, the history, the curse—it all vanished, and there was only the warmth of his touch, the pull between them that she couldn't ignore. Her breath hitched again, but this time it wasn't fear. It was longing.

"You don't have to face it alone," Liam whispered, his eyes burning with something raw and honest. He took another step closer, his body nearly pressed against hers now. "I'll be here, whatever happens. I won't leave you."

Ava's heart stuttered. She could feel it now—the weight of the promise in his words, the truth in his eyes. It was a promise that felt both like salvation and a trap. She wanted to believe him. She wanted to let herself fall into the comfort of his presence, to let him carry her through the chaos that had become her life. But there was always that gnawing question in the back of her mind: Could she trust him? Could she trust herself with him?

"Liam…" Her voice was barely a whisper now, fragile in the face of the storm swirling inside her. "What if the curse is already too much? What if there's no way out of this?"

His gaze darkened, and for a moment, she could see the pain that flickered behind his usual calm. But it was gone in the blink of an eye, replaced by a quiet determination. "There's always a way out," he said, his voice like steel. "But you have to want it. You have to choose it. And I can't make that choice for you."

Ava took a shaky breath, her mind racing. Choose. The word hung in the air between them, thick and heavy. She was being forced to make decisions she wasn't ready for—about her bloodline, about the curse, about the way Liam made her feel.

"You're asking me to choose between you and…everything else," she whispered, barely able to get the words out. "Between the curse and you."

Liam's expression softened, and he reached for her, his hand cupping her face gently, his touch both tender and filled with longing. "I'm not asking you to choose me over the curse," he said softly, his voice almost a whisper against the backdrop of the storm. "I'm asking you to choose the truth. To choose yourself—and to choose us."

For a moment, Ava felt as though she might collapse from the weight of his words. Everything—everything she had known, everything she had been running from—was now being laid bare, as if the truth had found her whether she was ready for it or not.

She closed her eyes, her breath shaky, and leaned into his touch, feeling the warmth of his hand spread through her skin, melting away the fear that had gripped her heart. In that moment, it felt like time itself slowed, and the world outside disappeared, leaving only the two of them standing there in the silent intensity of the storm.

Her lips parted, and for the first time, she allowed herself to speak the words that had been swirling in her chest, the words she had been too afraid to admit. "I don't want to lose you," she whispered, her voice barely audible.

Liam's expression softened, and his thumb gently stroked her cheek, his touch a balm against the turmoil inside her. "You won't," he whispered back, his lips just inches from hers. "I won't let you."

And then, as if there were no other option, as if the storm

and the curse and the world outside no longer mattered, Liam closed the distance between them. His lips brushed against hers, soft at first, tentative, but then deeper, more urgent, as though everything in him needed this. Needed her.

Ava's heart raced, her pulse thundering in her veins as she responded, her hands finding his chest, pulling him closer. The kiss deepened, slow and aching, as if they both had waited a lifetime for this moment, and yet, it still wasn't enough. She felt the weight of the curse, the promise of the truth, the inevitability of everything that had led them here, but in his arms, in this kiss, she found a moment of peace.

For a few breathless seconds, there was no curse, no bloodline, no dark legacy. There was only them—only the beating of her heart, the warmth of his hands, the promise that, whatever happened, they would face it together.

And then, just as quickly as it had come, the kiss broke. Ava pulled back, her chest heaving, her breath shallow. She felt disoriented, as if the world had shifted beneath her feet, and she was standing on the edge of something she couldn't fully comprehend. But even in the haze of uncertainty, she knew one thing: Liam was her anchor.

"You don't have to face this alone," he repeated, his voice hoarse now, his forehead resting against hers. "Whatever happens, we're in this together."

Ava nodded, her eyes closing for a moment as the weight of everything settled on her shoulders. She wasn't sure what the future held. She wasn't sure she was ready to face whatever truth was waiting for her. But with Liam by her side, she felt, for the first time, like she had a fighting chance.

And that, she realized, was the only thing that mattered.

Nine

The Heart's Choice

The night had settled in deep, wrapping its cold fingers around the mansion like a shroud. Ava could feel the weight of it pressing against her chest, thick and suffocating, as if the walls themselves were closing in. The storm outside had intensified, the wind howling through the trees like a warning, the flashes of lightning illuminating the darkened landscape with stark, jagged brightness. Yet, inside the mansion, the air was still—heavy with the silence that had followed their kiss.

Ava stood by the tall, dust-covered window, her fingers grazing the cold glass as she watched the world outside. The rain slanted downward in sheets, the light from the candles flickering in the distance, barely illuminating the garden, where shadows danced with the wind's furious breath. She had always loved storms—loved the way the world seemed to quiet itself, retreating into an unspoken, primal energy. But tonight, the storm felt different. Tonight, it felt like a reckoning.

She glanced back at Liam, who was sitting on the worn leather chair across the room, his gaze fixed on the fire in the hearth, the flickering flames casting shadows across his features. Ava couldn't read him. He had been distant since their kiss, his eyes shadowed, his expression unreadable. She could feel the tension in the air, like an invisible thread pulling taut between them. The storm outside echoed the storm inside her. She couldn't understand why she felt torn—torn between what her heart screamed for and the doubts that gripped her like ice.

Liam had warned her before. He had spoken of choices, of consequences, but there was something deeper now. The curse—the bloodline—everything was converging in a way she couldn't escape. The mark on her palm burned again, the familiar pulse of heat rising beneath her skin. It felt alive. It was alive, demanding, pushing her toward something she wasn't ready for.

"I don't know what to do," she whispered into the stillness, the words barely escaping her lips as she turned toward him.

Liam's gaze snapped to hers, his eyes dark and filled with something she couldn't quite place. He was standing now, moving toward her with the quiet grace of someone who had been waiting for this moment. The flickering firelight caught the edges of his features, casting shadows that deepened the storm of emotion in his eyes.

"You don't have to decide everything at once," he said, his voice low, almost too soft. He reached her and stopped, just within arm's reach. His breath, warm and steady, brushed against her skin, but there was a distance in his eyes. "I won't force you, Ava. Not now, not ever. This is your choice."

Her heart ached as she looked up at him, the vulnerability in his eyes taking her breath away. The weight of his words hung between them like a fragile thread—an unspoken promise that was both comforting and terrifying. He was giving her a choice, but could she make the right one? Could she choose him? Could she choose this life, this fate, and everything that came with it?

"I don't know what the right choice is anymore," she admitted, her voice shaky. "I don't know if I can keep living with this—this curse, this bloodline. But I don't want to lose you, Liam."

Her words were a confession, the raw honesty between them slipping out like a hidden truth she had been too afraid to voice. It was in that moment, as their eyes met, that she realized something fundamental: she was already bound to him. And no matter how much she tried to fight it, the truth was undeniable.

Liam's hand reached out, cupping her cheek gently. The warmth of his touch sent a jolt through her, his fingertips tracing the curve of her jaw in a tender gesture that belied the storm of emotions behind his eyes. He leaned in, his breath mingling with hers, and for a fleeting second, she felt as if time had stopped. There was only the two of them—the fire, the storm, the curse—all of it fading into the background as they stood on the precipice of something far more powerful than either of them could have imagined.

"You won't lose me," Liam whispered, his lips brushing against her ear. "I'm not going anywhere."

Ava's heart pounded. She closed her eyes, leaning into his touch, her pulse racing in response to the proximity of his body, the heat of his breath. But even as she felt herself melting into him, the weight of the decision still lingered, heavy and inescapable. The curse was a shadow hanging over them, a darkness that stretched back through generations.

Liam pulled back just slightly, enough to look at her, and in the dim light, Ava could see the conflicted emotions flashing across his face. He was holding back something, she could feel it—something raw, something painful. But he wasn't speaking, wasn't offering the comfort she so desperately craved. She had known from the beginning that he was bound to this curse, but now, standing so close to him, she realized just how deeply it ran through him.

"I need you to tell me something, Liam," she said, her voice small but firm. "I need you to be honest with me. About everything."

He hesitated, and for a long moment, neither of them spoke. Then, he nodded, a single motion that seemed to carry the weight of all the unspoken words between them.

"I can't protect you from everything, Ava," Liam said, his voice low, almost regretful. "The curse—it's a part of who we are. It's part of me. But I don't want it to be the end of us."

Ava's breath caught in her throat. "But how can we ever escape it? How can we ever be free?"

Liam's gaze softened, and for the first time in what felt like forever, a flicker of hope passed through his eyes. "You are the key, Ava. You always have been. The curse can be broken, but it's going to take everything. Everything we are, everything we have."

Her pulse raced as she tried to make sense of his words. You are the key. The words echoed in her mind, filling her with a sudden, dizzying sense of purpose—and dread. She could feel the mark on her palm again, its presence like a fire, burning with purpose, pulling her in.

Ava took a shaky step back, her mind whirling. "What if I can't do it? What if I can't break the curse? What if—"

Before she could finish, Liam reached out, gently pulling her back toward him. His hands were firm but gentle, like a lifeline.

"You can, Ava. I believe in you," he said, his voice thick with emotion. "But you have to believe in yourself. This is your choice, and I will stand by you, no matter what."

His words struck her like a blow to the chest, and for the first time in what felt like forever, she understood the weight of his promise. It wasn't just about the curse, or the bloodline, or the darkness that haunted them both. It was about them—about the choice to stand together, to face the unknown side by side.

Ava closed her eyes, breathing in deeply, the weight of everything finally settling in. She didn't know what the future held. She didn't know if she could ever break the curse, or if she even had the strength to face the darkness that awaited her. But in this moment, with Liam's arms around her, with his promises whispered into her ear, she knew one thing.

She couldn't face it alone.

With a deep breath, she pulled away slightly, her eyes meeting his, full of determination. "I'm ready," she whispered. "I'm ready to face it. Whatever it takes."

Liam's expression softened, his lips curving into a faint but real smile. "Then we'll do this together. I promise you."

The storm outside raged louder, the wind howling, the sky flashing with lightning. But inside the mansion, in the heart of the darkness that had consumed them both, there was a flicker of light. A spark of hope. And Ava knew, deep down, that together, they could face whatever came next.

Ten

Breaking the Chains

The air inside the mansion felt thick with anticipation, as though the very walls were holding their breath, waiting for something that had long been inevitable. Ava could feel it, too—an electric charge running through her, buzzing in the tips of her fingers and the back of her neck, making her heart race in her chest. The fire in the hearth crackled loudly, the only sound in the otherwise still room, its orange glow dancing across the stone walls, casting fleeting shadows that seemed to shift with each passing second.

She stood in the center of the room, her palms slick with sweat as she tried to steady her breath. The weight of everything that had led her here—the curse, the bloodline, the dark legacy she was bound to—seemed to hang in the air like a storm, heavy and oppressive. She could feel it all, pressing down on her, suffocating her, and yet there was a strange kind of peace in the silence. It was the calm before the storm, the quiet realization that she was no longer running, no longer pretending she could escape the truth.

Ava glanced over at Liam, who stood by the door, his figure cast in the shadows. His face was grim, his eyes fixed on her, though she could see the tension in the lines of his jaw and the rigid set of his shoulders. He was standing like a man on the edge of something—something dangerous, something that could break them both.

"I didn't think it would be like this," she whispered, her voice barely audible above the crackling of the fire. "I didn't think the curse would be… this real."

Liam's eyes softened as he stepped toward her, the shadows melting away from him as he approached. He reached out, his hand brushing against her arm, his touch warm and grounding.

The connection between them felt almost too intense, as though the very air between them was charged with the power of everything they had already shared—and everything they were about to face.

"It's real, Ava," he said, his voice low and steady. "But you're stronger than you know. And you don't have to face it alone."

Her heart stuttered in her chest at his words, the promise they carried. She didn't know how he could be so certain, so calm in the face of the uncertainty that threatened to overwhelm them both, but something about the way he spoke, the way he stood by her, made her believe in him. Believe in *them*.

"I'm not afraid of the curse," Ava replied, her voice steady now, though her hands were trembling slightly. "I'm afraid of what it's going to do to us. To *you*."

Liam stepped closer, closing the distance between them until there was nothing left but the heat of their bodies, the soft, steady beat of their hearts in the space between them. He cupped her face in his hands, his thumbs brushing against her cheek as he searched her eyes for something—perhaps reassurance, perhaps the same courage that he had always seen in her, even when she couldn't see it in herself.

"You don't have to protect me, Ava," he whispered, his voice thick with something she couldn't quite name. "You don't have to carry this alone."

She swallowed hard, the knot in her throat tightening as the weight of his words pressed down on her chest. She wanted to tell him everything—that she was terrified, that she didn't know if she was strong enough to face whatever was coming. But instead, she closed her eyes and leaned into his touch, allowing herself to surrender, if only for a moment.

Ava knew there was no turning back now. The mark on her

palm burned, the familiar pulse of heat spreading through her veins like wildfire, but it wasn't just the curse that called to her. It was the choice—*the choice* she had to make.

And in this moment, she made it.

"I'm ready," she said, her voice steady, but filled with an emotion she couldn't quite contain. "I'm ready to face it. To break the chains."

Liam's grip on her tightened slightly, his fingers digging into her skin as though trying to pull her even closer, as though he were afraid that if he let go, she would slip away from him. His face was inches from hers now, his breath mingling with hers in the space between them. He didn't speak immediately, but she could see the struggle in his eyes—could feel the way he was fighting against whatever fears and doubts were tearing at him.

"You don't have to do this, Ava," he said, his voice rough. "I can't ask you to—"

"You're not asking," she interrupted softly, her voice firm. "I'm choosing this, Liam. I'm choosing you. I'm choosing *us*."

The words hung in the air between them, fragile but undeniable, like a thread woven into the very fabric of their fates. And when Liam kissed her then, it wasn't gentle or soft—it was fierce, urgent, as though this moment was the only thing that mattered. She kissed him back with everything she had, her hands fisting in the fabric of his shirt as the heat between them flared, a burning desire that refused to be extinguished.

For a brief moment, the world fell away. There was only the press of his body against hers, the fierce connection between them that no curse, no bloodline, could sever.

But as the kiss deepened, as the passion flared between them, Ava felt it—the unmistakable presence of something darker, something *foreign* that cut through their closeness like a jagged blade.

A sudden, cold wind swept through the room, the door slamming shut with a force that rattled the windows. Ava pulled back from the kiss, gasping, her chest heaving as she looked around, her pulse racing.

Liam's eyes were wide, his jaw clenched as he took a step back, his body tense. He turned toward the shadows, his senses alert, as though he could feel something shifting in the air. Ava followed his gaze, her heart thundering in her chest as she tried to make sense of the sudden change.

"*It's happening,*" Liam muttered, his voice tight with urgency. "*It's already started.*"

Before Ava could ask what he meant, the ground beneath them trembled. A low, resonant sound filled the air—like the echo of a drumbeat, deep and thunderous, shaking the walls of the mansion.

"What is that?" Ava whispered, fear creeping into her voice as she instinctively stepped closer to Liam.

"It's the curse," Liam replied, his voice tense. "The chains are breaking. *You're the key,* Ava. You have to stop it."

Ava felt the mark on her palm flare to life, the heat intensifying until it was unbearable. She cried out, stumbling back as the pain shot through her veins like fire. She fell to her knees, clutching her hand, the heat too much, too overwhelming. The world around her seemed to spin, the shadows closing in as a dark figure emerged from the corner of the room, its form indistinct, like a silhouette caught in a fog.

Liam knelt beside her immediately, his hands gripping her shoulders as he tried to steady her. "Stay with me, Ava. You have to fight it. Don't let it consume you."

But Ava could feel it—the darkness, the weight of the curse trying to pull her under. The force pressing against her chest, trying to break her, trying to drown her. It was too much. She couldn't breathe. She couldn't—

Suddenly, the pain in her hand *exploded*, and with a fierce, defiant cry, Ava's body jerked upright. Her hand shot out, the mark burning like a brand, and with it, the darkness recoiled. The room went still, as if everything had been held in suspension, waiting for her to make the final move.

She looked up at Liam, her breath shallow but steady now. The room had returned to normal, the fire crackling in the hearth once more, the air still and silent.

Liam's eyes were wide as he stared at her, his lips parted as if he couldn't believe what had just happened. "Ava..." he whispered, disbelief lacing his voice. "You did it."

Ava slowly looked down at her palm. The mark was gone, the pain fading into nothingness, and in its place was a faint, glowing warmth. A feeling of relief. A sense of freedom.

She had broken the chains.

And with that, she realized something even more important— *they had won.* Together.

Liam reached for her, his hands trembling as he gently cupped her face, his eyes searching hers, still in awe. "You're incredible," he said, his voice thick with emotion.

Ava smiled softly, the weight of everything she had endured lifting off her shoulders. "We did it," she whispered, her voice barely audible, but filled with the certainty of what they had just accomplished.

And as they stood there, the storm outside subsiding, Ava knew that nothing—no curse, no dark force—could ever break what they had

Eleven

The Final Hour

Ava's breath hung in the still air, each inhale sharp, each exhale trembling as she stood before the ancient altar. The stone was cold beneath her fingers, slick with an otherworldly chill, as if the very earth around her was steeped in forgotten secrets. The flickering light from the torches lining the walls cast long, twisted shadows that stretched into the far corners of the room, dark shapes that seemed to move as if alive. It was as though the entire world had paused—waiting for something. Waiting for her.

The chamber was vast, its high ceiling arching overhead, lost in shadow. The air smelled faintly of incense, a rich, heady scent that stung her senses and clung to her skin. The stones beneath her feet were uneven, worn from centuries of use, the ancient markings etched deep into the surface telling stories of those who had come before. Those who had sought answers, or perhaps something far darker.

Ava's fingers brushed over the symbols etched into the altar, the cool stone beneath her touch seeming to hum, vibrating with a power she could almost taste. The mark on her palm pulsed again, the familiar heat rising to a fever pitch. It was like a beacon—demanding, pulling her toward the ancient ritual she had been destined to complete.

Behind her, Liam stood silently, watching her, his presence an unspoken promise. He had been with her through the darkest moments, standing by her side even when the world seemed to crumble around them. The storm outside had intensified again, the wind howling against the walls of the old stone building, a constant reminder of the battle they had fought to get here.

"You don't have to do this," Liam's voice broke through the thick silence, a quiet plea laced with concern. "Ava, if there's any other way, we can still walk away from this."

She turned her head, catching his gaze. His eyes, dark and filled with an intensity that matched the storm outside, searched hers, as if he could find the answers he needed there. There was something raw in his expression—something vulnerable. She could see it. She could feel it.

But there was no turning back now.

"I have to," Ava whispered, her voice tight with the weight of the words. "This is the only way. The curse... it's been waiting for me. For my bloodline. And now... now I have the chance to end it."

Liam stepped closer, the sound of his boots against the stone floor muted by the tension that crackled in the air. His hand reached out, his fingers brushing against hers, and the simple touch sent a jolt of warmth through her, grounding her, reminding her of everything they had fought for. Everything they had fought against.

"I'll be right here," he said, his voice low, steady, but thick with emotion. "You don't have to do this alone, Ava. You never have."

Ava swallowed hard, nodding, though her throat was tight with emotion she could hardly process. He was her anchor in this storm, the only constant in a world that had shifted beneath her feet. But the path she had to walk—they had to walk—was one she had to face alone. The curse had been her inheritance. And only she could break its chains.

The altar in front of her seemed to pulse, its markings glowing faintly as the ritual began. Ava could feel the air growing thicker, the very room itself pressing in on her as the power of the ancient magic began to awaken. She could hear it now—the hum beneath the stone, the whisper of something old and dark, like the very earth was calling to her.

She looked down at her hand. The mark was alive now, glowing faintly beneath her skin, rippling with power. It was no longer just a symbol. It was part of her—her blood, her soul—and she could feel it now, the connection to the curse that had plagued her family for generations.

Liam's voice broke through the reverberations of the magic. "Ava—"

She didn't turn. She couldn't. There was a sharp pain in her chest, a twisting knot that she had felt growing since the moment she had agreed to this—since the moment she had accepted her fate. But there was no other choice. She had to face it. She had to end it.

Without a word, she stepped forward, her feet moving as if guided by something beyond her control. The room seemed to open up before her, the altar ahead, waiting. As she neared it, a shadow moved in the far corner of the room. Ava froze. The figure emerged from the darkness, its presence like a cold wind that swept through the room. A woman, her face obscured by a dark veil, her presence ethereal and terrifying.

Ava's breath caught in her throat. It was her. The woman from her past, the one who had haunted her dreams. The one who had whispered the curse into her bloodline.

"You're too late," the woman's voice echoed in the chamber, cold and final. "You think you can end what was never meant to end?"

Ava's heart pounded in her chest, her mind racing. The woman was the embodiment of everything she had feared—of everything her bloodline had been cursed to face. But this time, Ava would not back down.

"I will end it," Ava said, her voice stronger now, the words cutting through the tension in the air. "I choose to break the chains. This ends tonight."

The woman's lips curled into a smile, a cruel twist of her mouth. "You don't get to decide, child. The curse belongs to all of us. To your blood. To the darkness that runs through you. You can't escape it. You will never escape it."

Ava clenched her fists, the power from the mark on her palm flaring once more, the heat shooting up her arm and spreading through her chest. The woman's words were nothing more than echoes now, fading into the distance as Ava stepped forward, toward the altar, toward her fate.

With a force that felt like the very earth itself shifting beneath her, Ava reached out and placed her palm against the altar's cold surface. The mark burned hot beneath her skin, a pulse of energy that surged through her veins, filling every part of her with an unbearable heat. She could feel it now—the darkness, the legacy of the curse, all of it flowing into her, feeding her, pushing her toward the very edge of herself.

Her body trembled as the power inside her built, swelling until it felt like it would tear her apart. The shadows in the room seemed to twist, writhing with dark energy, but Ava didn't pull away. She couldn't.

And then, with a final, desperate cry, she released everything. The power surged outward, and for a moment, the room was bathed in brilliant light, blinding and pure. The mark on her palm flared brighter than ever before, casting out the darkness that had haunted her bloodline for so long.

The world seemed to shudder, as if it was being torn in two. The woman's scream filled the air, but it was quickly drowned out by the force of the magic Ava had unleashed. The ground beneath her feet cracked, the altar shaking as the chains of the curse that had bound her family for generations were shattered. Ava felt the weight lift from her chest, the air growing light and free as the darkness receded.

And then, as quickly as it had come, the light faded. The room grew still, the air thick with the aftermath of the battle that had just been fought. Ava stood there, gasping for breath, her heart pounding in her chest, her hand still resting on the altar. She could feel the power still humming beneath her skin, but it was different now. It was no longer a curse. It was a part of her, but it was no longer in control.

She turned, her legs weak beneath her as she faced Liam. His eyes were wide, his expression a mixture of awe and disbelief. But beneath that, there was something else—a sense of relief. A sense of freedom.

"You did it," he whispered, his voice hoarse. "Ava… you did it."

Ava's heart thudded in her chest as she stepped toward him, her body trembling with the weight of everything that had just happened. She reached out, her fingers brushing against his, and when their hands touched, it was as though the world had come back into focus. The curse had been broken. The chains had been shattered.

"I couldn't have done it without you," Ava said, her voice thick with emotion, her eyes meeting his with a mixture of exhaustion and something deeper—a quiet promise.

Liam pulled her into his arms, his hold strong and reassuring as she buried her face against his chest. The room around them was silent now, the storm outside fading into nothingness as the dawn began to break, a soft light creeping in through the cracks in the stone walls.

The curse was broken. And together, they had faced the darkness and survived.

And for the first time in a long time, Ava felt free.

Twelve

A New Beginning

The air was thick with the scent of rain as it fell in sheets, cascading down the windows of the mansion. It was no longer the fierce storm that had raged through the night; now, it was a steady drizzle, soft and cleansing, as if the world itself was trying to wash away the remnants of the battle they had fought. The sky beyond the window was a dull gray, the clouds hanging low like an endless stretch of uncertainty. But inside, the room was quiet, peaceful—still.

Ava sat by the window, her fingers tracing the cool glass, watching the rain blur the world beyond. Her thoughts felt just as fogged, like she was still caught in the echo of everything that had happened. The power she had unleashed, the curse broken, the weight of it all still settling into her bones. She had thought that once it was over, once the chains were shattered, she would feel lighter, freer. But now, sitting in the quiet aftermath, the space around her felt too empty, too silent.

Her body still hummed with the residual energy, but it was no longer chaotic, no longer oppressive. The power had been released, the darkness had been driven out, but the light that followed was blinding. Ava wasn't sure who she was anymore—not just because of the curse but because of everything that had happened, everything she had learned, and everything she had chosen.

A gentle tap on the door broke her from her thoughts. She turned her head, her gaze still distant, but when the door creaked open and Liam stepped inside, she felt her heart skip a beat. His silhouette in the doorway was a presence she could never ignore, his aura always so strong, so steady. He was the anchor in the chaos, the only constant in the world that had constantly shifted beneath her feet.

His eyes met hers, and for a moment, neither of them spoke. There was a silence between them—an understanding that hung in the air, thick with the weight of everything they had just been through. He stepped closer, his movements slow, deliberate, as though he were afraid that if he moved too quickly, the world would fall apart.

"How are you feeling?" he asked, his voice soft, his concern hidden behind the strength that always seemed to surround him.

Ava's lips parted, but the words caught in her throat. She didn't know how to answer. How could she explain what she felt? How could she put into words the strange emptiness that lingered, the aching need for something that she wasn't sure how to name?

"I'm not sure," she replied finally, her voice just above a whisper. "I feel… lighter. But also… lost."

Liam nodded, as if he understood exactly what she meant. He came to sit beside her, the warmth of his body a quiet comfort against the cold chill that still clung to her skin. For a long moment, they sat in silence, just the soft sound of the rain against the windows and the occasional crackling of the fire in the hearth. The weight of the moment hung in the air, and Ava felt herself slowly, gently drawn into Liam's presence, as if she had been holding her breath for too long and finally, she could release it.

She turned toward him, her heart beating a little faster as their eyes met. He was so close now, so close that she could feel the warmth of his breath on her skin, feel the steady rhythm of his pulse just beneath the surface. Everything about him—the calmness, the steadiness, the way he seemed to wrap the world in the palm of his hand—drew her in.

"I don't know what's next," she said softly, her gaze dropping to her hands, her fingers resting in her lap. "After all of this, after breaking the curse… I don't know where to go from here."

Liam's hand reached out, his fingers brushing against hers with a gentleness that took her by surprise. The contact sent a shiver through her, a warmth flooding her veins that had nothing to do with the lingering power. His touch was steady, reassuring, and it brought her back to herself, back to the moment.

"You don't have to know," he said, his voice low, but firm. "Not yet. We'll figure it out together."

Ava turned her hand, letting their fingers intertwine. The simple act felt like a promise, like an unspoken vow that the storm had passed and they would face whatever came next side by side. The world outside was still filled with uncertainty, but in this moment, there was only the two of them.

She looked up at him, her chest tight with something she couldn't quite understand. "What if it's not enough? What if we're not enough?"

Liam's gaze softened, the lines of worry around his eyes easing slightly as he leaned closer, his forehead resting gently against hers. "Ava, we're already enough. You *are* enough. You've always been enough. You just have to see it."

His words cut through the doubts that had clouded her mind, and she closed her eyes, letting them settle into her heart. The weight of everything she had been carrying—the burden of her family's legacy, the darkness that had threatened to consume her—was still there, but now, it was lighter. It didn't control her. And as she breathed in deeply, letting the scent of the rain and the fire fill her lungs, she realized that she no longer had to carry it alone.

The tension that had been building in her chest slowly unraveled, and she allowed herself to lean into him, letting the warmth of his body surround her, chase away the cold that had taken root in her bones. There were no more lies, no more secrets. Just this moment. Just the two of them.

"I don't know what the future holds," she said, her voice muffled against his chest. "But I know I want to face it with you. With you by my side."

Liam's arms wrapped around her, pulling her closer, his embrace a comfort that she never wanted to let go of. She could feel the steady beat of his heart, the warmth of his body, the certainty in the way he held her. It was the first time in a long time that she felt at peace, that she felt like she was exactly where she was supposed to be.

"And I'll be right here," Liam whispered, his voice a promise against her hair. "I'm not going anywhere. Not now, not ever."

Ava closed her eyes, letting his words wash over her like a balm, soothing the last of the lingering doubts in her mind. Together, they had faced the darkness. Together, they had broken the chains. And now, in the quiet aftermath, there was nothing but the possibility of a future they would build together.

The rain outside continued to fall, the storm finally abating, and for the first time in what felt like forever, Ava felt like she could breathe again. The curse was broken. The past was no longer a weight around her neck. And as she sat there, with Liam's arms around her, she realized that the future was wide open—full of uncertainty, yes, but also full of hope.

And in that moment, with him beside her, she knew she had everything she needed to face it.

www.ingramcontent.com/pod-product-compliance
Lightning Source LLC
LaVergne TN
LVHW020931200726
843506LV00011B/1926